curiouʂabout

MARS

BY RACHEL GRACK

A M I C U S • A M I C U S I N K

What are you

curious about?

CHAPTER THREE

What We Might See on Mars

PAGE

14

Curious About is published
by Amicus and Amicus Ink
P.O. Box 227
Mankato, MN 56002
www.amicuspublishing.us

Designer: Aubrey Harper
Photo researcher: Bridget Prehn
Editor: Gillia Olson

Library of Congress Cataloging-in-Publication Data
Names: Koestler-Grack, Rachel A., 1973- author.
Title: Curious about Mars / Rachel Grack.
Description: Mankato, Minnesota : Amicus/Amicus Ink,
[2022] | Series: Curious about outer space | Includes
bibliographical references and index. | Audience: Ages
6-9 | Audience: Grades 2-3 | Summary: "Questions
and answers about Mars' appearance, features, and
missions encourage inquiry-based learning for curious
early elementary-age readers. A Stay Curious! Learn
More feature models research skills and doubles as a
mini media literacy lesson. Includes quick facts chart,
infographics, glossary and index"– Provided by publisher.
Identifiers: LCCN 2019046645 (print) | LCCN
2019046646 (ebook) | ISBN 9781681519739
(library binding) | ISBN 9781681526201 (paperback)
| ISBN 9781645490586 (pdf)
Subjects: LCSH: Mars (Planet)–Juvenile literature.
Classification: LCC QB641 .K62 2022 (print) | LCC
QB641 (ebook) | DDC 523.43–dc23 LC record
available at https://lccn.loc.gov/2019046645
LC ebook record available at
https://lccn.loc.gov/2019046646

Photos © NASA cover, 1, 3, 14–15, 15 (inset, Mars);
NASA / Dave Williams and Jay Friedlander 2 (left), 4–5;
NASA / JPL-Caltech / MSSS 2 (right), 12–13; NASA /
Science Photo Library 6 / JPL-Caltech 7; Alamy; Science
Source / Detlev Van Ravenswaay 8; NASA / JPL 9;
Getty / Dneutral Han 11; NASA / Goddard Space Flight
Center / Reto Stöckli 15 (Earth); Shutterstock / Dima Zel
17 (bottom); NASA / JPL-Caltech / University of Arizona
17 (moons); Science Source / Mark Garlick 18–19;
NASA / JPL-Caltech / MSSS / Texas A&M Univ. 20;
Shutterstock / Daryaart9 21

Why is Mars red?

Mars is named for the Roman god of war. Its red color reminded people of war.

The dirt on Mars is full of rusty iron dust. Winds kick up the dust and blow it around. This gives Mars a reddish color. People call it the Red **Planet**. Up close, Mars also looks brown, gold, and tan.

What's that huge scratch?

An illustration shows what it might be like at the edge of Valles Marineris.

That scratch is the longest **canyon** in our **solar system**! Valles Marineris runs for 3,000 miles (4,800 km). That's the whole United States from east to west. Its deepest spot is four times deeper than the Grand Canyon. Imagine standing at the edge. Yikes!

Olympus
Mons

Does Mars have mountains?

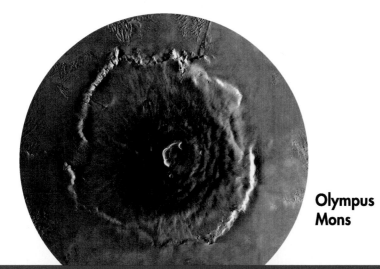

**Olympus
Mons**

Yes! One of them is also the biggest **volcano** in the solar system. Olympus Mons is really tall and really wide. Mars' volcanoes haven't erupted for a long time. Scientists think the last blast was a million years ago.

Olympus Mons Compared to Earth's Tallest Mountain

Olympus Mons:
14 miles (22 km) high

Mount Everest:
5.5 miles (8.8 km) high

CHAPTER TWO

When did we discover Mars?

People could always see Mars in the night sky. Mars looked like a red star. The color made people curious. Egyptians mapped its path 4,000 years ago. People later found out it was a planet, not a star. In 1609, Galileo was the first to look at Mars with a **telescope**.

Mars is seen in the sky above Cologne, Germany, on the night of a lunar eclipse. ⟶

Have people ever visited Mars?

NASA's Curiosity rover takes a selfie on the surface of Mars.

Not yet. But Mars may be the first planet people visit. It's close to Earth. No other planet has been studied more. Today, six spacecraft **orbit** Mars. Several **rovers** have explored on land. People could be next!

DID YOU KNOW?

Sending spacecraft to Mars is tricky. Almost half of all Mars missions have failed.

Could people live on Mars someday?

An illustration shows what living on Mars might look like.

Scientists think so! **Astronauts** will go first, though. They must wear spacesuits. We cannot breathe the air. It's usually very cold, too. To live there, people need a power source for air, water, and food. They will use sunlight to make electricity for power.

COMPARE YOUR WEIGHT

On Mars, you'd weigh a bit more than 1/3 your weight on Earth.

 = 50 lbs (23 kg)

= 19 lbs (8.6 kg)

Earth   Mars

Does Mars have moons?

Yes, it has two. But no one knew about them until 1877. They were too small to see! Phobos circles close to Mars. It's slowly getting closer to the planet. It crosses the sky every four hours! Deimos looks more like a star in the Mars sky. This **moon** is slowly drifting away.

Manhattan Island

Deimos

Phobos

DID YOU KNOW?

Phobos is just a little larger than Manhattan Island in New York City. Deimos is about half that size.

Does Mars have any storms?

An illustration shows an approaching dust storm on Mars.

Mars has huge dust storms. Some last weeks and cover the whole planet! The biggest one we know of was in 2018. Dust blocked out the sunlight. This caused problems. Remember, power there comes from the Sun. One rover lost all power and died.

What is a day like on Mars?

Sunrise and sunset on Mars can look blue!

A day on Mars lasts a little over 24 hours. That's very close to a day on Earth. The daytime sky would be hazy orange. At sunrise and sunset, the color around the sun would be blue! At night, you could see tons of stars.

QUICK ANSWERS

Place: 4th planet from Sun

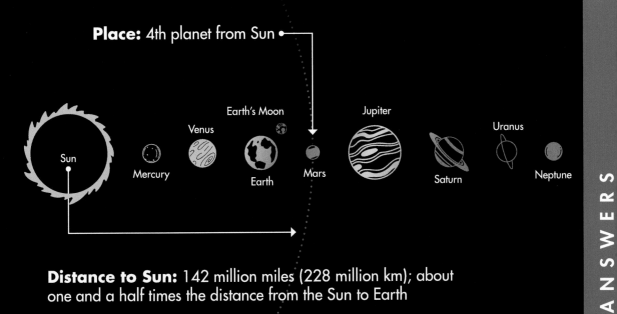

Sun

Mercury

Venus

Earth's Moon

Earth

Mars

Jupiter

Saturn

Uranus

Neptune

Distance to Sun: 142 million miles (228 million km); about one and a half times the distance from the Sun to Earth

Revolution / Length of Year: 1.8 Earth years ●→

Rotation / Length of Day: 24 hours, 37 minutes

 **Temperature:** average of -81 °F (-27 °C)

Diameter: 4,212 miles (6,780 km); about half the diameter of Earth

Earth   **Mars**

ASK MORE QUESTIONS

What do rovers learn on Mars?

Would you want to live on Mars?

Try a BIG QUESTION:
What could living on Mars teach us about living on Earth?

SEARCH FOR ANSWERS

Search the library catalog or the Internet.
A librarian, teacher, or parent can help you.

Using Keywords
Find the looking glass.

$\mathcal{Q}$

Keywords are the most important words in your question.

?

If you want to know about:
- rovers exploring Mars, type: MARS ROVERS
- what it's like to live on Mars type: LIVING ON MARS

FIND GOOD SOURCES

Here are some good, safe sources you can use in your research.
Your librarian can help you find more.

Books

Discover Mars by Beth Georgia, 2019.

Living on Mars by Ellen Lawrence, 2019.

Internet Sites

NASA: The Mars Rovers

spaceplace.nasa.gov/mars-rovers/en
NASA is the space program for the U.S. government. It's a great source for space information.

TED-ed: Could we actually live on Mars?

ed.ted.com/lessons/could-we-actually-live-on-mars-mari-foroutan
TED-ed is a non-profit educational site with videos on many topics.

Every effort has been made to ensure that these websites are appropriate for children. However, because of the nature of the Internet, it is impossible to guarantee that these sites will remain active indefinitely or that their contents will not be altered.

SHARE AND TAKE ACTION

Find Mars in the night sky.
Ask a parent to use a free stargazing app on their cell phone or use a telescope.

Join an astronomy club.
If there is not a club, start one! See if a teacher will help.

Plan a Mars movie night.
Do the movies get anything right about what it would be like on Mars?

GLOSSARY

astronaut A person who travels to space.

canyon A deep, narrow valley.

moon A large object in space that circles a planet.

orbit To circle around something.

planet A large, round object in space that circles a star.

rover A spacecraft with wheels used to explore on land.

solar system The Sun and all objects in space that circle it.

telescope A long tube with eyepieces that makes faraway objects seem larger and closer.

volcano A mountain that blasts hot gas and lava out of its top.

INDEX

About the Author

Rachel Grack has been editing and writing children's books since 1999. She lives on a ranch in Arizona. The desert offers spectacular views of the night sky. Rachel and her family set up the telescope and enjoy evenings of stargazing. They especially like zooming in on the Moon and planets.